Looking at Birds

Contents

The Blackbird 2
The Black-Headed Gull 4
The Blue Tit 6
The House Sparrow 8
The Pied Wagtail 10
The Robin 12
The Starling 14

Written by Hilary Minns and Mike Torbe
Illustrated by Andrew Midgley

KELSEY PRIMARY SCHOOL

Collins Educational
An Imprint of HarperCollinsPublishers

THE BLACKBIRD

How it behaves
Dashes across the garden or the road, flying very low. Feeds on the ground, on grass or under bushes, throwing leaves aside to look for food. Hops and runs, gets panicky, and flies off quickly.

What it looks like
Male bird is black with a golden beak. Female is brown.

What it sounds like
Blackbirds call *chak-ak-ak-ak* or *pink-pink* when they are scared.

Where to look for it

You will see blackbirds in gardens and parks. The male sings from a high place like a chimney or the topmost branch of a tree.

Something to look out for

When the blackbird hunts for worms, it cocks its head on one side so it can see the ground clearly. When it lands, it flicks up its tail. In spring, listen for its beautiful song sounding a bit like a flute.

The blackbird's story

One spring two blackbirds built their nest on top of the hinge of the door to the playground. The caretaker locked the door so no one could open it by mistake, and everyone used another door. The children liked to watch the parent birds feeding their babies after the eggs hatched. In a few weeks, the blackbird family flew away.

THE BLACK-HEADED GULL

How it behaves
Lives in flocks. Always on the lookout for food. Chases after other gulls and tries to take their food. Has a quick pattering run. At night, flies to nearby water where it's safe from foxes.

What it looks like
Dark hood in summer. A mark behind the eye in winter. Red legs and red beak.

What it sounds like
The black-headed gull gives a raucous scream of *kraah*.

Where to look for it
You will see black-headed gulls near rubbish tips, lakes and canals and on school playing fields and playgrounds.

Something to look out for
In the winter these gulls line up along school roofs waiting for the bell to go. When the children go inside, they eat the food that's been dropped on the playground.

The black-headed gull's story
A flock of black-headed gulls saw a hedgehog coming near their nests to steal the eggs. Some of them attacked it from the air and others attacked it on the ground. They hit it with their feet and beaks, and some of them splattered it with their droppings! The hedgehog went away without its dinner.

THE BLUE TIT

How it behaves
Flits from branch to branch, always on the move. Small groups call to each other.

What it looks like
Small. Light yellow underparts and bright blue cap.

What it sounds like
The blue tit calls *chick-a-dee-dee-dee* or *tsee-tsee-tsee-tisisit*.

Where to look for it
You will see blue tits in trees and bushes in gardens, parks and in the countryside, eating caterpillars, greenfly and other small insects.

Something to look out for
Blue tits hang upside down when they feed. In the autumn and winter, they come to bird tables to eat nuts and fat.

The blue tit's story
A blue tit once learned how to peck through the silver top of milk bottles to get at the cream. That was when most people had milk delivered in bottles. Soon many blue tits picked up the trick and stopped at houses to have some cream. Now that more people get milk in paper cartons, the blue tits no longer come round for their drink.

THE HOUSE SPARROW

How it behaves
Usually in flocks of three to ten. Come right up to you for food, but always seems to be on the lookout. All fly away if they get suspicious. Fight other sparrows in the spring. Crouch on the ground and have dust baths in the summer.

What it looks like
Small, brown bird. Male bird has a black bib.

What it sounds like
The sparrow chirps a loud, short, single note sounding like *cheep!*

Where to look for it
You will see the house sparrow low down on the ground near buildings or hedges, or near people who are feeding them.

Something to look out for
Young sparrows beg for food from their parents. They crouch low and pretend to be helpless.

The house sparrow's story
House sparrows usually build their nests of woven grass and straw in holes under the roofs of houses. However, when motorway service stations were first built, they gathered there because of the food left around. The sparrows couldn't find holes for their nests because most service stations were new, so they made their nests in the trees nearby. They went back to the ways of sparrows long ago, before there were cities or houses.

THE PIED WAGTAIL

How it behaves
Wags its tail up and down when it lands. Walks, makes a short run and then wags the tail again. Flies up and circles, then lands again, singing as it does.

What it looks like
Small black and white bird with long tail and delicate, thin legs.

What it sounds like
Wagtails make a twittering sound that comes out as *chizzick*.

Where to look for it
You will see pied wagtails around school playgrounds or any stretch of grass or open space.

Something to look out for
In the autumn and winter, wagtails might roost in very large numbers. Sometimes they roost near water, sometimes in trees and on buildings.

The wagtail's story
Every morning a pied wagtail sat on the wing mirror of a car in the school car park. The bird leaned over and attacked the image in the mirror, thinking it was an enemy. After a few days, the wagtail had made a mess on the car. The teacher who owned the car got cross. So she made little covers to put over the mirrors. The bird stopped coming because it thought it had frightened away its enemy!

THE ROBIN

How it behaves
Stands up very straight when looking at something. Fights other robins who come near, except for its mate and its young.

What it looks like
Small brown bird with a red breast and a red face. Thin beak and spindly legs. Young birds are speckled brown all over.

What it sounds like
In summer, the song starts high and gradually gets lower. When scared, robins call *tic-tic* or *tic-ic-ic*.

Where to look for it
You will see robins in parks and gardens, on the ground or in hedgerows, or sitting on tree branches.

Something to look out for
If you dig your garden, a robin might come very near, even on to your spade handle. It is looking for things to eat as you turn the soil. In winter, listen for a quiet, sad song.

The robin's story
A robin came into the same garden every day. The family who lived there started feeding cheese to the bird. It became very tame and used to hop into the house to be fed. When it mated, the robin stayed nearby, building its nest on a shelf in the lean-to outside the back door.

THE STARLING

How it behaves
Always in gangs on the lookout for something to eat. All swoop down together and squabble over food. Bully other birds. In the evenings, gather together in large flocks.

What it looks like
Middle-sized bird. Appears black, but feathers are metallic green and purple on close sight. Young starlings are brown.

♪♪ **What it sounds like**
Starlings sing unmusically, chattering and whistling *seeeooo!* They also copy sounds, including other birdsongs.

Where to look for it

You will find starlings everywhere in town and country and in the city centre, especially in winter. They sometimes sit on chimney pots.

Something to look out for

Starlings roost noisily together, sometimes in thousands. Sometimes they meet on telephone wires, pylons or fences, and then fly to their roost together, making large swirling patterns in the air.

The starling's story

A large flock of starlings roosted on the ledges of a building in the city centre. Their droppings and their noise bothered people. Everyone tried getting rid of the birds. People put sticky paint on the building. They taped the sound of frightened starlings and played the tape to scare the roosting flock. They even sent tame hawks, the starling's enemy, to attack them. Nothing worked.

Glossary

delicate
flimsy and frail-looking
flit
to move quickly and lightly
metallic
shiny, like metal
raucous
loud and harsh
roost
to rest and sleep; also the place where birds rest and sleep
squabble
to quarrel noisily
topmost
at the very top
twittering
making a quick, light, high sound

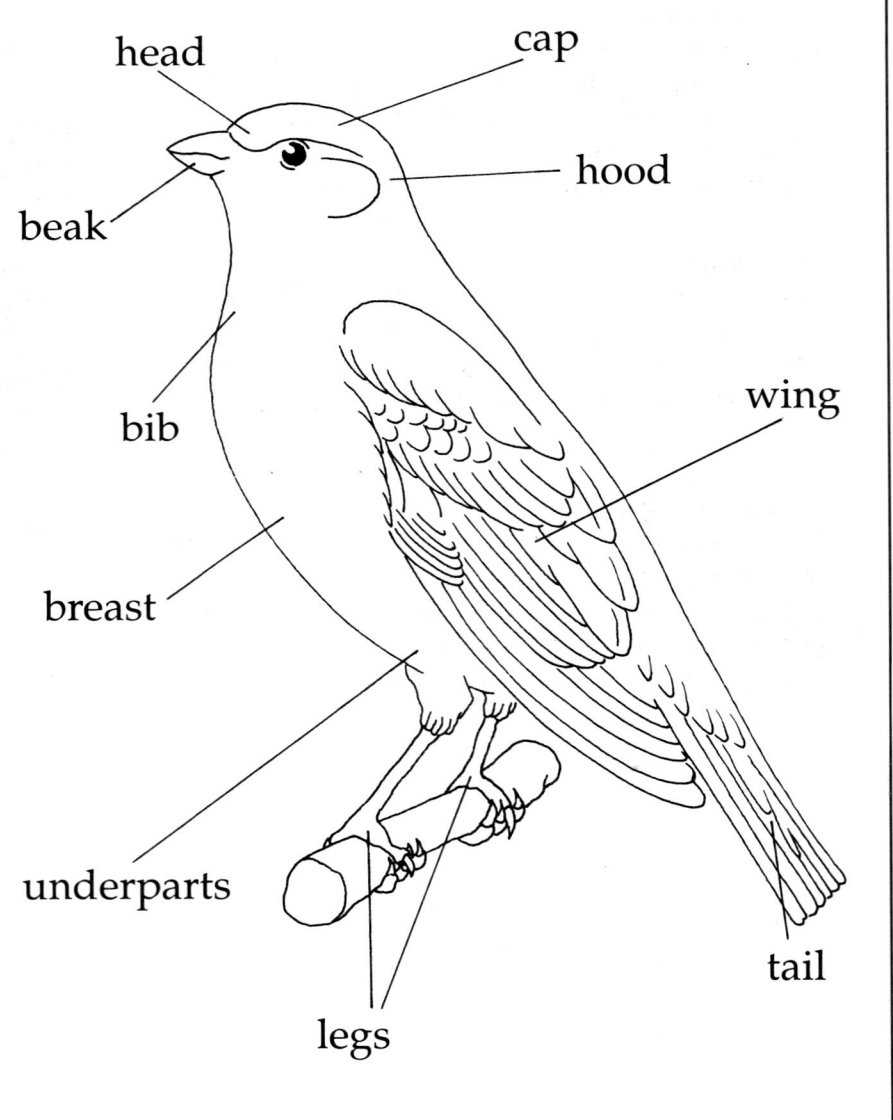